*For Lucinda*

## La Soupe et les Nuages

Ma petite folle bien-aimée me donnait à dîner, et, par la fenêtre ouverte de la salle à manger, je contemplais les mouvantes architectures que Dieu fait avec les vapeurs, les merveilleuses constructions de l'impalpable. Et je me disais, à travers ma contemplation: 'Toutes ces fantasmagories sont presque aussi belles que les yeux de ma belle bien-aimée, la petite folle monstrueuse aux yeux verts.'

Et tout à coup je reçus un violent coup de poing dans le dos, et j'entendis une voix rauque et charmante, une voix hystérique et comme enrouée par l'eau-de-vie, la voix de ma chère petite bien-aimée, qui disait: 'Allez-vous bientôt manger votre soupe, sale bougre de marchand de nuages?'

Baudelaire: *Petites Poèmes en Prose*

# CHRISTOPHER REID

## *Pea Soup*

Oxford   New York

OXFORD UNIVERSITY PRESS

Oxford University Press, Walton Street, Oxford OX2 6DP

London  Glasgow  New York  Toronto
Delhi  Bombay  Calcutta  Madras  Karachi
Kuala Lumpur  Singapore  Hong Kong  Tokyo
Nairobi  Dar es Salaam  Cape Town
Melbourne  Auckland

and associates in
Beirut  Berlin  Ibadan  Mexico City  Nicosia

Oxford is a trade mark of Oxford University Press

British Library Cataloguing in Publication Data
Reid, Christopher.
Pea soup.
I. Title
821'.914    PR6068.E426
ISBN 0-19-211952-4

Library of Congress Cataloging in Publication Data
Reid, Christopher.
Pea soup.
I. Title.
PR6068.E426P4    821'.914    82-6294
ISBN 0-19-211952-4    AACR2

Set by Rowland Phototypesetting Ltd.
Printed in Great Britain
by J. W. Arrowsmith Ltd., Bristol

# Contents

## Pea Soup

A hecatomb;
haruspication of pods . . .
It is thus that we understand
our kitchen gods –

workaday hierophants,
opening each green victim
with a neat jab of the thumb,
cascading entrails

(like so many plump suspension-dots)
into a deep pan.
Our recipe book
is the Book of Fate,

to be interpreted wisely
and with some imagination.
The shiny china look
of a raw hambone,

the floe of fat
you scrape with a tablespoon
from quivering stock,
one moment's ghost of salt

and a wincing lemon
must all be rightly noted.
The gods are not mocked!
We are expected

to follow their fickle games,
before launching
our rich domestic cargo
upon those blue, blustering flames.

## Fête Champêtre

This bourgeois clematis-bower
might be a wallpaper by Vuillard –
pink stars jotted down
on a dense scribble of green –

or some high, abrupt stage-flat,
hands have heaved out
to signify the end of the garden.
The annual rustication

of our indoor properties
proceeds, with random babies,
a quorum of florid aunts,
help and hindrance

over the tea-things. We carry
Windsor chairs in our oblationary
stagger across grass. A white cloth
flares, undulates, lacks breath,

then subsides to a wonky plateau,
on which, like billets-doux,
minute sandwiches are to convey . . .
But listen: here comes a tray

of china cups, pale bone,
absorbing the unaccustomed sun
and celebrating with a feeble
percussion. Hardly audible,

somebody lingering indoors
extorts a few bars
from the dud piano – a perfect
prelude to whatever next.

# A Metaphysical Outrage

Enter a beaming moon-head.
The body follows,

a miniature shuffling tide;
an afterthought, like the trailed

tail of a capital Q
in some dab hand's florid

and sentimental script.
Eyes on the baby

read her, read her for new signs,
as though this meagre tadpole-meteor,

so fervently hurtling
across our sitting-room floor

might tell us the secrets
we yearn to take account of.

But what can a single
errant letter spell?

Presuming to snatch
a heavenly entity

from its highway,
I find it a mundane planet, rowdy

with tempests, floods and unwelcoming quakes;
a furious, opaque vowel.

## On a Postcard

Vermeer's Dutch thusness,
and a young woman exploring
the landscape of a keyboard
with plump fingers:
so light fell, one feels,
and became paint.

A more awkward business,
ours here. Despairing
of a cluttered cupboard,
baffled by anger's
exigent protocols,
we could not say what was meant.

Yet some things have a point:
unopened daffodils,
with their necks like flamingos';
a dull coin recovered –
accidents conferring
art's oddness and justness.

# A Parable of Geometric Progression

The white pretext
for a solemn Tudor dance;

lax, then tautening;

a hammock or cat's cradle
in some playground game-by-rote

of mirror-meeting,

concession and goodbye;
a grave suspense between us;

folding, folding –

this washed and ironed double-sheet
diminishes by halves.

Time brings us, darling,

to such pristine slabs
and a turf-stack of fresh towels . . .

A week-end's washing

crowds about our furniture,
an orderly débris,

as I sit here, knotting

socks into boxers' fists.
How patiently you tangle

with wry triangles, clothing

the family of nobodies
who loiter in our dark.

# A Lesson from Cookery

But is it anything
more than the fury
of lobsters thrashing
against death's pot-lid?

Our egos in armour –
the dark clamps down
and we celebrate
the will to survive.

A fit of resistance,
then the battle resolves itself:
shrieking steam
and the legendary blush.

A German painter
of macabre inspiration
embarrassed his *Creation*
with a boiled *homard*.

# Magnum Opus

A figment: a cathedral.
Approaching it, I found
that scaffolding fuzzed the steeple.
The austere limestone, stained
by moss-blob, lichen-dapple,
commanded ambiguous ground.

Pigeonholed for resurrection,
pious mannequins took the sun.
A huge and implausible fiction –
yes, but I dipped in
for cursory inspection.
The organ droned on.

A token midmorning sunlight
pewtered the plain glass
of one aloof transept.
Bells were delirious,
blurbing God's handsome construct,
the tall tale of the cross.

So, jubilantly pillared –
reading from left to east –
the story seemed straightforward:
earth's multitudes effaced,
bar a putative few transfigured
in the windows of the blest.

But then there were digressions
and subplots for the dead.
Certain august persons
struck attitudes. Children hid.
Two briefly-married cousins
prayed side by side in bed.

A waxy marble bishop
savoured his ambience
of echoes, irony, gossip:
a narrative opulence,
leading one on to worship
through shadows and ample hints.

Hewn down in some thug battle,
the great knight slept. His scars
were tourist penknife doodles.
He lacked nose and ears.
At his feet, a wounded beagle;
behind him, six hundred years . . .

The organ, modulating
on currents of reverie,
seemed like accommodating
all secularity,
with grave rumpuses, flytings
of fanfares and fugal whoopee,

when the frilly choir entered,
blasé and epicene.
I recall a young woman who fainted,
my neighbour's atonal keen
and the brute baby that ranted
against the preaching dean.

# Charnel

God's clownish, tumbling bells
bang out their Sunday-morning scales
with rabble-rousing eloquence.
But what of the sad, cramped hells,
we know lie hidden hereabouts?
Minded by corpulent nymphets
with wings and frowns, in reticence
they guard their deeply embedded doubts.

A mawkish exercise,
but one that everyone enjoys –
to step about this cluttered suburb
like a daytime ghost. We scrutinize
indifferent marble garden art,
whilst only our near neighbours, inert,
ignore the bells' blithe hubbub
and resolutely stick apart.

Confronted by so much stone,
the irony of the autumn sun
would make light of the whole affair,
*pace* that smothered undertone.
But reading of what we lack
in unknown names, quaint rhetoric,
how can we fail to despair
amid death's haphazard bric-à-brac?

In church, stout men at ropes,
gargantuan pan-pipes
and a bible-bolstering eagle –
props to abash our lapsing hopes –
contrive to adumbrate
a world of pastoral joy. Discreet
chorales endorse the beadle,
who gathers cash on a wooden plate.

Ineffectual routines . . .
'Get up, you lazy bones!'
is what the bells say every Sunday,
and a nosegay by a headstone means
much the same. As though
there was something we might yet do,
to assuage the *contemptus mundi*
of those who bide their time below . . .

# Scottish Themes

### Iona

Home baking is a feature . . .
And someone has flattened
both abbots and soldiers
to gingerbread-men.

Innumerable kings
lie tucked away here
under these jagged
tablets of black fudge.

St Martin's biscuity cross
stands nearby.
The tourists are ravenous . . .

### Caithness

Gaunt stones like well-women,
with urns on their heads,
invigilate the graves
of the northern dead.

Ranked all weathers
in a hillside pen,
they stand at attention
like too many chess-men,
an *embarras* of queens.

## Melrose

Gargoyles are nosy,
but see as little as we do:
only black stones
with their skulls and crossbones.

I preferred the nameless
blocks in the mason's yard –
discreetly edged
with rosettes, ivy-leaves, crowns;
as neat and as glossy
as the choicest boxes
in a Piccadilly sweetshop.

# Cambridgeport Christmas

Ice aches and eases
underfoot:
a luscious pleasure
for the solitary walker,
where morning flings its shadows,

extravagant and pat,
across playground and parking-lot.
Cars are stunned
by a Yuletide smother-love.
Bushes weigh

their meted dollops,
and the boxy clapboard churches
are drenched and cleansed
by a piquant light from the east.
One for every block,

they favour a dapper
domestic garrison air.
Time now to register
pangs of accord
between each yearning object

and its heaven-sent word,
before cars cough and lurch to life,
dislodging snow,
and churches receive
their annual revellers,

the strenuous, frowning carollers.

## Our Host Speaks

Fog can cancel most things.
The water corrodes.
We are lucky still to be here
in this temporary city,
where windows are defended
by filigrees of dwindling rust,
and minor marine gods bleach and eat
the barn-doors of palazzi.

The old stone blots and softens.
Our citizens promenade
like ghosts apprehended through drizzling twilight
on marble veined and stained
by ancient seepings. This tessera crumbles
like a block of cork,
while others are vellum, buff, steak-red
or spattered like quails' eggs.

We delight not just in surfaces,
but in their relinquishment as well.
Walls flake like bark.
Rope grows a waterlogged mane
and lions modify
their evangelical features.
You can grey your fingers
on the dust of endless eponymous saints.

The priests make an oriental sound,
droning, gonging the echoes off
celestial domes in mordant pleasure.
Churches dock
close to the pink and ochre squares
where pigeons gather
like applicants for the post of Holy Spirit,
or a drowned Christ hangs out to dry.

You must let me show you
the tiny boudoir-church
that is my favourite,
with its touch-worn Ovidian altar-frieze.
Here satyrs, popping pods, bull-tritons, leaves,
the innocent raptures of sexy mermaids,
flourish from marble. And heaven itself
is graced by an off-centre patch of damp.

## So Much to Read, So Little to Understand

Pisces, or yin and yang, the fish
in Mrs Tanaki's porchside pool –
flushed by its faucet waterfall –
were corpulent, a pinky beige,

marinading, as if in a dish,
with less meaning than the obscure
labels affixed to the jamb of her door.
I thought how print on a Japanese page

fell like branches of her weeping willow.
A cemetery two gardens away
was packed with planks: enormous, written-on

tongue-depressors. But what did they say?
Names? Prayers? The carp in their shallow
basin might have known once, then forgotten.

# Three Sacred Places in Japan

## Practical Zen

Hush. Timber-smells. The grain and sheen
of floorboards buffed by unshod feet.
A dim chamber with its paper screen
and brisk ink-daubs, where the abbot sat . . .

This small pavilion affords
a full view of two cosmic gardens:
here, gravel combed like a placid sea
and set with islands of rude stone;

there, undulant moss as terra firma.
I thought that I was quite alone,
until I saw the apparition –

a monk with meditative murmur
bowing his bristle-stippled head,
to cull weeds from their dusty bed.


## A Complex Sentence from the Envoy's Memoirs

I met the obscure god
of their trumpery summerhouses
in a dank shed by the lake
with its mad square-dance of midges,

where dragonflies, stunned and coupling,
hovered above dead pads
and torpid subaqueous fronds,
and I looked into his bronze,

bucket-smooth face to find
some sacrament of the mind
that transcended all clutter and swelter,

but nothing gave, and I left him,
smugly beatitudinous,
alone on his artichoke throne.


## Itsukushima

On guard against the harbour fish,
a dozen anglers line the quay.
Rowboats, a few feet out to sea,
moored empty, shrug their bafflement.

Big barrel-drums, salt-seasoned wood
furnish apartments of the shrine
that's built on stout piles like a pier:
I see the point of worshipping here.

Below, the tiny tender crabs
tango in shallows, risking land,
then dashing to sockets of sludged sand.

Green seaweed wraiths, a beer-can, drunk,
are tugged by the tide . . . You Nothings, bless
me in my next-to-nothingness!

## Kawai's Trilby

Cold comforts of a hotel room:
the air-conditioning and fridge
join forces for a chummy hum,
barbershop-style. Poised on the edge
of bed, I think how far I've come.

Two weeks ago we kissed goodbye.
Now in a towerblock hotel
in a strange land, I inventory
the trappings of my pilgrim cell:
bath, holy scriptures, a TV.

Outside my window, a huge sign
flushes, then cancels – Op and Pop
apotheosized! Brisk neon
routines jolly the cityscape,
like the desk-toys of businessmen.

I saw them from the penthouse bar
this evening, while musak thrashed
its pandemonium by my ear.
Symplegadean ice-cubes clashed
in a Scotch sea. I nursed a tear.

Maudlin without you, in a world
lacking all reciprocity,
I watched the emblems as they twirled,
the brand-names blinking, and briefly
felt the dull fear of a lost child.

An apprehension of Japan,
vertiginous and mad! I knew
the swimminess of limbo then,
its throb of silence, and missed you
to make sense of the things I'd seen.

*An ancient blotched and fissured rock,*
*eminent on a pile of cushions.*
*Two toddlers playing shuttlecock.*
*Raw fish. The pavement urinations*
*of spruce old men. Crows in the park.*

*Yellow lizards in a glass jar*
*in someone's window. Tasselled lanterns*
*at shrines, restaurants – everywhere.*
*The tedium of civic fountains.*
*Kawai's trilby. Harbourside deer.*

Memories occupy my mind
like bright lights in an urban void:
symbols you may not understand
when I report them; yet a word
in earnest may at times transcend . . .

Thousands of miles from you, I slip
my clothes off. Bed–lamp lit, these sheets
look fresh as a new envelope.
I'll turn the hot tap till it blurts
and drums the tub, for fellowship.

## Numen

In winter, sequestered ground:
the city's forgetting-place
for a mathematics that failed.

Yet some ideas have taken root,
disjunct, inchoate,
the tokens of a possible eloquence:

ribs of a tilted cone,
the three dimensions caged for climbing
and a slide's collapsed radical sign.

Then, if you are lucky,
you may catch the *genius loci* –
a muffled hobgoblin in Wellingtons and peaked hood –

riding the same arc back and forth;
who would like to animate the lot,
though this must do for the time being.

# Dark Ages

This is our heraldry of dirt:
a dog crappant on a lawn vert.
A supermarket-till cartouche
looping inanely through a bush
must have been threaded by some child.
No civic wall but is defiled
by spraygunned mottoes, jousting cocks –
the clichés of the heterodox.

Stepping warily through the park,
a constable like Joan of Arc
obeys the rasp of airborne voices.
Headscarved old women, breaching buses
like siege-troops, go to their crusades
of shopping in the far arcades.
A bollard and a station-wagon
have met like St George and his dragon.

Wind blows to make the rubbish rage,
impotent in its public cage,
or take tithes from the estate trees.
A page of news enfolds my knees,
supplicating. God bless the fierce,
string-belted mendicant who stares
where someone's frenzied tights and pants,
pegged to a maypole, dance and dance!

# Disneyland

## In the Gardens of Spain

I saw him from my window –
preposterous matador,
flaring and vibrating
at his dowdy paramour.

The faded banderillas
planted in her head
were turned to him in profile:
she was cutting him dead

with her dawdling indifference,
as Io once snubbed Argus,
unmindful of the dark eyes
and aggressive susurrus.

His huge, lurching fan
agitated the air
like the Furies in possession
of a wickerwork chair.

But those shimmying side-feathers
of tawny apricot,
the empurpled royal blue
about his serpentine throat,

all the fuss and fandango
were wasted on that hen.
He packed up and departed.
I have seen him since then

on the apex of our roof,
a far-fetched weathercock.
And at times, by day and night,
his impassioned squawk –

like the amplified awakening
of a raucous oboe-reed –
will penetrate the house
to remind us of his need.


### The Cows Come Home

Scuffed, ancient luggage,
our far-travelled cattle
sashay to the gate
in Indian file,
squelching through paddies
of feculent mud.

They have lain all day
in the obdurate perfume
of the midden-field
like odalisques,
nonplussed by the absence
of their handsome sultan.

Nude, aloof,
there they paddled their ears
and switched their tails,
haphazardly despatching
the little black slaves
that danced attendance
on errands of defilement
and circuitous rumour.

Florrie, Dulcie,
come home from your dream
of discontent!
We will love you here
for yourselves alone,
you exuberant, care-laden,
carnal hussies.

## Aquarius

A pod, a purse, a penknife –
and whatever they contained –
the ju–jus of the underworld
hung behind glass windows,
waiting to be explained.

Fauve in the murky water,
of course, they were simply tropical fish,
on wings of pantomime gauze
levitating
in accordance with certain arcane laws.

This crab, an Indian goddess,
safe in her battery of arms
(bracket folding upon bracket),
preserved her edible secret
against the lobster's farcical alarms.

But everything was bogus:
flapping a great sheet,
the ray rose up like a revenant
and showed his underside,
where human features could just be descried.

Your dear, departed uncle
trying to 'come through'
turned out to be a turtle,
the old buffoon of the zoo,
and not drowning, but waving . . .

With aerials for whiskers
attuned to the voice of God,
the giant catfish looked as fat
and smug as the fish in the proverb,
that swallowed the cat.

# Uncle Wally Remembers Africa

The king came
to his own sacrifice
on a silver litter
with cushions of ice.

A quilted armour
of dull gold
covered him amply.
Only a bold

topknot of dry leaves
thrust from his crown,
grey-green and jagged.
We set him down,

then carved him in slices.
How we enjoyed
that fibroid flesh,
those lurking juices!

# Ivesian Fugue

The string quartet
at our fête champêtre
revealed such fierce sonorities –
*Bonk, bonk, bonk!* –
that I stopped to consider
how music springs from catgut,
and four men bobbing
and scuttling on a lawn.

# The Ambassador

Life in this narrow neck
of the galaxy reads like a rebus –
one damned, inscrutable
poser after another.
The planet surface is cluttered
with objects: wherever my feet fall,
something gives like a gibus
or jumps away with a squeak.

Impossible to tell,
as it were, between living and dead.
An innocent-looking box
will suddenly burst one side
with garish laughter. From hiding
behind a babel of bricks,
a three-inch ladybird
creeps out on stridulant wheels.

Most of the populace
turn out to be ciphers, dummies,
mere animalcules of stuffing
and stitching. I talk to them
politely, but they, it would seem,
are determined to say nothing
(although, if you press their tummies,
some do make a querulous noise).

And so I follow a nervous,
diplomatic course:
keeping my counsel; listening;
attending rigid tea-parties
with mad-eyed plastic beauties
and blotto frogs; whispering
and peering in through the front door
of the tiny bourgeois palace . . .

If I lose my patience,
forgive me. Yesterday
I kicked a troop of saluting
soldiers down the stairs;
but at heart I still adhere
to the maxim, that through a studious
reading of chaos we may
arrive at the grammar of civilization.

# The Inspector

Ah, the baroque sexuality
of our public-garden sculpture!
The old king sits on his high-buttocked horse,
a cupid tumbles a dolphin
at the very brink of a fountain
and something has nibbled Pomona's nose.

The profligacy of autumn
has advanced too far to be halted now,
and yet an obstinate boatman
still punts the wrong way through dry leaves,
cussed, slow, methodical,
like Charon transporting his phantom dead.

These conker-caskets, ransacked,
sink beneath waves of leaves –
a treasury of untold regrets.
But don't stoop; one simply lets them go
with yesterday's smutted papers
and that sky of sliding clouds.

Our people like to have things orderly:
thus, the man who whacks his thigh
to recall a vanishing terrier,
that skips away like his own renegade,
Gogolian moustache.
Will he ever teach his new dog the old tricks?

In this playground of impromptu metaphors,
a fierce eremite, attentive
to the baragouin of ducks,
tosses them manna of sliced bread,
as though he were the only god
to a tribe of rancorous dodgem-drivers.

I recommend that we fix
some centre to cosmos and chaos.
A bulldozer to these romping stones!
Imagine a high-toned statuary
of minimal symbolic clutter,
with its fine proportions and right lines.

## Bathos

Yes, I had come to the right place: the jumbo
cheeseplant languishing at a window told me,
and the lift's bisecting doors confirmed it.

Emboxment and apotheosis followed
at once. I approved the fragrance of a late
cigar, while numbers counted themselves discreetly.

Time to remember the whole of my wasted life:
evenings of apathy; vague, extravagant walks;
the cat bemused by my keyboard melancholias.

And now this feeling, as if I had been deftly
gathered into an upward oubliette,
to arrive – where? – at a meadow of sulphurous carpet.

There was a young girl at her desk with three
telephones. I spoke to her politely. Magic!
I heard: 'Mr Dixon will be with you shortly.'

A huge vase full of plastic flowers stood
on a ledge, where an old man, passing, bent to savour ther
The unregenerate minutes turned and turned.

Of Mr Dixon's office, I can recall
the photograph of his wife, some freckled apples
and an alarming stuffed owl under its bell-jar.

But everything else has vanished. Stepping out
of the lift, beyond the ailing cheeseplant, I
looked back and wondered if something important were
    missing.

## Business as Usual

Flashing their lamps by daylight,
the police are like Diogenes
in full cry after an honest man:

engines and high-toned sirens,
one moment here with their moral furor,
the next, ostentatiously gone.

Drawn to my upper window,
I can see how the grim, ornate façades
of office, consulate, bank –

the Empire's hortatory architecture –
continue to expound
their well-weathered formulations

re the bleak black blank.
A torrent on a flagpole
in Heraclitean flux

animates one febrile theory,
whilst, on a pediment below,
three young girls kitted-out in Vestal dress

pose endlessly for a photograph –
with cold shoulders to the wind's ravings!
Detailed to represent

the Banking Virtues, they brood
over the doughty growth of men's savings
and cannot be persuaded to laugh.

# Latin American

The cocktail guitarist's
more numerous, but vaguer, fingers
do poignant, flim-flam things
to somebody's taut
and apprehensive heart-strings.

Abetted by the pulse of bongos,
a muted trumpet's gloats and smarms,
the adroit lover
shuts his eyes to woo
the woman, wooden in his arms.

Trashy, but somehow true,
the things he tells her.
With understanding he palpates her neck.
We see his urgency edge lower,
the plectrum peck . . .

Tropical humours!
The old untamed romance!
This piano is a holster for music.
Microphones hide
in a jungle of pinguid rubberplants.

I thrill to the shush of gourds,
that coconut clopping
and our prestidigitant gigolo,
with his hair brushed like a new LP
and one toe-cap hopping.

## Pastoral

The barmaid applepicks
her glasses off the rack.
She pumps and pumps for beer –
a thin pizzle-dribble.
Only a quarter past six,
and business is still slack
in this London country pub,
where the only customer
apart from us
is an old military dandy
of the most cultivated sort.
Spruce in his Seurat tweed
and fresh graphpaper shirt,
he douses his double brandy
with a brief siphon-snort,
then sets to wooing the barmaid
over her no-man's-counter
with forays of cavalier banter.
A hanky swells from his pocket
to tell her his heart overflows,
but he might as well dally for windfalls
from the fruit-machine
for all the interest she shows.
Her white hair is blue –
a bland Impressionist cloud –
and next to the empty beer-crates
lives a poodle, topiaried,
that the old gentleman hates.
Bottles hang upside-down,
their spirits sinking
at so much heavy drinking,
while tankards, pot-bellied, on hooks,
are lords of the air and as free
as a flight of sitting-room ducks.

## Folk Tale

And then there was a mad astronomer,
the shepherd of a solitary moon,
who chased his tiny, pock-marked planet
over the hills for half a morning.

The countryside was his enemy:
uncouth heather and highwayman copses
kept taking his jewel and hiding it.
His only friends were the eighteen pickpockets.

Once he ambled into a nostril
of sand, that sneezed and sneezed to expel him.
He left wounds on grassy pelts
and green tonsures. He often drew mud.

From time to time, coming upon
the moon, diffident, snug as a mushroom
on dank turf, he'd take his club
and smack it back into the sky.

It must have had occult properties,
to have led him so gullibly over the hills
in his houndstooth cap and tweed knickerbockers,
feinting vague arcs in the moist air.

# The Portrait Game

(after Turgenev)

I

A florid old cherub,
the Silenus of a library –
its most benign spirit.
He comes every day,
huffing and shuffling.
You hear him round the corner,
when forgetfully he whistles
two soft watery notes.
In love with books, he clambers
perilous toy steps
to pluck the furthest prizes,
the heaviest and arcanest.
Volumes loll where he's been.
Spreadeagled on the top
of a mahogany cabinet
(like a tomb for gilt folios),
a lexicon lies open:
with his fulvous middle finger
he strokes its cleft.

2

I don't like the look
of this fellow.
He ought to be jolly,
but in fact he's a bully,
pettish, pampered
like a Roman emperor.
Nose as porous
as a sore old strawberry.
Lips, maroon and rubbery.
A challenging rhino's amble
to and from the table
where he drinks nine pints a night.

He tells his mates what's what,
and they laugh when he does.
Married? Never was.
Works as foreman
in a yard stacked with rusting drums –
most days by the gate,
tormenting his gums
with a chipped matchstick;
sulky, obtuse,
but quick to be sarcastic.


3
He's a farm–labourer,
a sturdy perfectionist.
Day after day he endures
the fug of the henhouse,
where he patiently rehearses
the complex gobbledygook
of his own new Hen Symphony.


4
In a gust of garlic,
Moroccan or Turkish,
the smug patron
of a Soho restaurant.
He runs it well,
with napkins as natty
as the headgear of nurses,
outlandish implements
for all our cack-handed
operations on snails.
He talks to every table,
condescending and banal.
If you ask for champagne,
he comes himself
to ease out the mushroom,
then shovel the bottle
back into its pail

of icy rubble.
He hardly ever smiles,
but, then, exactly
how many murders
have been committed
on the mere silent say-so
of those tawny teeth?


5

An abject busker,
though he was once a soldier,
who, in a seaport
near the Equator,
possessed a young girl
as glossy as an aubergine,
with a curious perfume
both fecal and sweet.
A cap like a puddle
now lies at his feet,
to receive the odd penny.
He wheedles his harmonica –
a horrible sound.

# The Traveller

First, I plotted my course
by all the wrong clocks of London,
the constellation of friends
whose secrets I alone could read,
hoping by venture to navigate
a route to the heart of the dream.

But you know how every dream
is apt to follow its own course.
I saw the great buses navigate
the capes and inlets of London
and tried in their commerce to read
some entente between my friends –

the archipelago of friends
that spattered, in my dream,
a map too dazzling to read.
I was always miles off course,
trusting to currents in London
that only a fool would navigate.

The eldritch gulls, who navigate
with their far-flung friends
the rowdy sea-air above London,
complicated the dream.
They were not lost, of course
(with an open city to read),

but anyone else could read
in their attempts to navigate
the diplomatic course
of conduct proper to friends,
a wild fear of the dream-
cartography of London.

Undaunted, I travelled through London
and, learning how to read
the prosy flow of the old dream,
I found that I could navigate
between clocks, buses, gulls, friends,
some kind of a course.

Dear friends, I had hoped in due course
to bring back my dream-map of London
for you to read and to navigate . . .

# The Naive Reader

She loved the big old novels:
*Jane Emberley's Affair*;
the Anatolian travels
of *Captain Matcham*, where
he lost his heart and reason;
*Truth* and *The Errant Season*.

She owned several hundred.
They lined up in her room
like caskets to be plundered
for rich words, the perfume
of antique paper and
the sheer weight in her hand.

The scuffed gold of their titles
to her meant country parks
and long family battles.
She knew the complete works
of Mrs Cattermole
as part of her own soul.

Massive, indulgent volumes
invited her to move –
a ghost amid double columns
and passages of love –
in a closed world of fine
feelings and grand design.

Following the ambagious
currents of Gothic prose,
traversing dappled pages,
she relished the brief throes
of fear, anger, desire,
that chance words would inspire.

But some could be confusing:
eclipsed by an oak door,
or earnestly perusing
thickets of metaphor,
she sensed she might find meaning,
but for their intervening.

Why, in the bonfire autumn
of *Ellencourt*, did they
trample Sir Harry Portman,
when he fell from his bay?
Why did the comic tutor
betray the milk-girl's suitor?

Why was the Provost angry?
Why did the wild friend ride
from Hamptonshire to Hungary?
And why was Tom denied
by Edith Cove, who knew
that all he said was true?

The interloping spirit
that gave each chapter life,
at times she could not bear it:
seeing the Arab knife
flare by the water-butt,
she clapped the plump book shut.

Yet, when she came back later,
there were the frowsty church,
the Biffins at the theatre,
long smears of silver birch
against the sky, that face –
each in its proper place.

For everything was written
and had to be obeyed.
A small part of the pattern,
like Fate or a housemaid,
she knew she must attend
until the very end.

## The Exotic Nouns

He knew he could not hope to dwell
where paragraphs are islands,
and yet he undertook the trip . . .

Touching at his first port of call,
he heard the garrulous saxophone
of a café band, and felt inspired
at once. The natives sipped
a cocktail, thick, but pétillant,
of apricot and grenadine,
which was highly alcoholic. They slept
most afternoons. Their skins
were cinnamon or a fair tan. One woman wore
a parrot like an acute accent
on her shoulder. He marvelled at
the angry gadget of its beak
and its shifty aplomb, before passing on.

The next place had a dusty road,
though not much else. A butterfly –
yellow, as big as a handkerchief –
blinked for a while in the trick haze,
then disappeared. But it was as if
he ought to have stayed for several days.

On the third island he met a man,
bearded like a Bellarmine jar,
loud-voiced and fond of flowers, who dealt
in contraband silver. He had a daughter.
Her name was Augustine.
Our hero dallied as long as he could,
following her through uneven courtyards,
across the tussocky orchard,
afraid of letting the words slip by
too soon. Fig-tree, anxiety, sunlight, baboon:
every noun was enchanting.

                         Poor fellow!
He knew he could not hope to dwell,
and yet, and yet . . .

# Borrowed Time

We swam in a pool
beneath magnified dragonflies.
Your Dutchman's pipe
waxed fat

by the verandah pillar,
dreaming its freckled
bell, like a saxophone
oozing into

efflorescence.
A peahen, crowned
to be Empress of India,
clattered on the iron

table. Rain,
and a caravan
of uptight guineafowl
sped by. The ground

was strewn
with ochre handaxes –
harder than ancient
poems – the basketwork

of yellow weavers
and, under a tree,
evidence for the massacre
of plums. Hoopoes.

Scampering ants.
A lime-green chameleon,
stretching from fence
to shrub in torpid

motion, beguiled us.
I saw a nibbling
bug, like the god
of a cool magnolia.

The jacaranda pods
were too stiff
to act as castanets.
How sad it was to leave!

# A Disaffected Old Man

The spider in her hanging theatre;
the patient villainy of cats:
the afternoon foretells disaster,
now we have time to sit and watch.

Outdoors, lulled by the sun, I berce
the sticky brandy in my glass
and contemplate the apple-tree,
that writhes like a family history.

My grandchildren are playing cricket
with a beachball and tennis-racket.
My ancient wife sits on my left.
Leaning, we kiss with cigarettes

to make a tremulous bridge for love.
This yawning book, its foxy breath . . .
I pluck out phrases like stubborn teeth,
only to mislay them – and soon enough.

Now yoked to her bib, a baby crawls
a number of yards, but then stalls,
seeing the next-door cat dash past
with his foolish, fat, feathery, false moustache.

# Logodaedalus

With cork paunch
and thatch of feathers,
the ever-optimistic phoenix
leaps up, prevaricates
and tumbles
between these children's
flurries and swipes.

Poor bird, netted
time and again!
A hurtling moppet,
a feather-brain –
yet you make them peer
into sunlight,
flinch at your high jinks,
then shy away.

The prestigious moments
we betray
return to taunt us:
words that might
with love's ingenuity
have flown right,
but fell to extinction –
ruffled, aghast.

A small dog dashes past,
like Atalanta
with her chewed ball
and sidelong scamper.
The children have such fun,
urging a giddy toy
towards the sun.

# Bravura Passage

I saw the Thames today,
that dismal river
with its vague waves
and petty froths.

The bridge I stood on
shuddered with a fever
of traffic, and the flags lacked
all flamboyancy.

Begrimed by obscure use,
otiose warehouses
shadowed the rigid,
corky bobbing of gulls.

In that waste of water,
the only unquelled spirit
was a motor-launch –
brisk, oblique

and abounding in chutzpah.
I thought of you
and your adventurous beauty
in the midst of things.

## Bucolic Interlude

From his high, shuddering seat,
the lordly fellow
who cuts and stripes
the Council's grass

surveys a terrain
of meticulous damage –
his job thoroughly done.
He cannot know

that you will come here later
like Ruth in her exile,
to kick the loose, lost stalks
and snuff up their spiciness.

# At the Wrong Door

A bank-manager's rapid signature
of hair on the bath enamel, twist
and tail, to confirm that I have missed
you by a minute; mat on the floor,

stamped vigorously with wet; your
absence palpable in the misty,
trickling, inexorcizable ghost
that occupies the whole mirror –

I cannot rub it away – the room
clings to me with such a perfume
of soap and sweat, that I can only

stop to think how somewhere else
you may be standing, naked, lonely,
amid a downfall of dampish towels.

## At the Kitchen Table

A master of Zen calligraphy,
never content, with my coffee-cup
I practise circles on the table-top:
a meditation on nullity,

or time by-passed. Now when shall I see
a resolution? A heavy drop
of water, pulsing to fall from the cold tap,
does, but another bulges promptly

to take its place. Some oranges
in a commune, like perfect strangers,
dwell upon their own navels,

untransformed. Not much to do,
but pinch these fiddly blue labels
from their skins, as I wait here for you.

## Zeugma

Is it foolhardy to hope
that by some ingenious trope
we'll widen, and not hamper, our scope?

I do not think so,
for there is a knack we know
involving both passion and punctilio.

We are two words set free
from the common dictionary,
to act with a new, *ad hoc* complicity.

Our only go-between, 'and',
carries its contraband
in a package the unpoetic may not understand.

# Acknowledgements

Acknowledgements are due to the editors of the following, in which some of these poems first appeared: *The Times Literary Supplement, New Statesman, Sunday Times, London Review of Books, The Honest Ulsterman, Kenyon Review, Bananas,* and the *Poetry Book Society Supplements* of 1980 and 1981. 'Pastoral' was joint winner of the Prudence Farmer Award in 1980, awarded annually for the best poem to appear in the *New Statesman*.